Autism for Life

Ian M Weller

Autism for Life

Contents

vi

Autistic for Life

April 2nd is Autism Awareness Day
for the majority of the world.

While April is also considered
Autism Awareness Month.

For people on the spectrum,
Autism is not for
one day or one month.

It's 24/7.
It is a life long journey.

As someone on the spectrum,
I have decided to be
a role model for the young.

It is a volunteer position
that doesn't pay.
But any hope given
to the parent or child,
Priceless.

I'm Autistic for life.
It's what I am,
and I wouldn't have it
any other way.

Brothers & Sisters

Attention to those on the Spectrum,
I have something to say to all of you.

Welcome to the family,
my brothers and sisters
of situation.

We are in a world
that doesn't understand
and possibly fears us.

The neurotypical elitists
would rather see us
fail and be inferior
than rise and thrive.

This world is a cruel place.
Like Rocky said,
it will beat you to your knees
and keep you there if
you allow it.

We must grow stronger
both in will and strength.

The ignorant
would lock us away
in an institution
or have us executed

for no reason.

Brothers and sisters,
I don't know
what kind of teacher
I am.

But I will gladly
give you the tools
to be better
than what they
want you to be.

Follow me.

Our Way

Get ready.
It's going to be
a very long road ahead.

We should not follow the path
those who don't know us
say we have to take.

If we did that,
we would all be locked up
in an institution
for life.

A waste of potential
that could one day
change the world.

There is no easy road
for people like us.
We forge our way.

We forge our way to
what makes us happy,
our dreams,
and more.

Don't be a stranger
to difficulty when it appears.
You beat it at least once already.

You can beat it again,
and as many times as it takes
to reach your goals.

Goals of happiness,
goals of dreams,
any goal before you,
you can make a path
to reach it.

That,
my brothers and sisters of situation,
is the way we win.
We make our way.

Marvel's Mutants and the Autism Community

Everyone has heard of Marvel Comics.

Everyone has heard of The X-Men.

Now, what if I told you
there is a variation of Mutants walking among you
as I speak?

At first, your skeptical.
You think
"There aren't any super powered people walking around."

I didn't say anything about powers.
I said a "variation" of Mutants.

Mutants in Marvel are looked upon with disdain.
Every normal person is afraid of Mutants
If they don't know anyone who is a Mutant.

The general population seek a way to be rid of Mutants,
or a way to make them normal people.

I know a special group of people
who fit this same scenario.

This scenario of fear and misunderstanding.
This group you undoubtedly heard of.

The Autism Community.

There are many groups of people who favor
or understand what the Autism Community

While there are many more who fear Autism
and are willing to do anything to eliminate
or give false hope that Autism is curable.

There is no need of a cure,
for there is nothing wrong with us.

If we receive the help we need early enough,
we can blend in and be a positive part of society.

The same way as the X-Men aid people in the Marvel Universe,
We can aid in our own way.

Give us a chance.

Learning to be Human

I'm living in a world
that is run by those who see
people like me
as possibly inferior,
or worse
less than human.

Most of the time
I don't care
what they think.
But I am forced
to play by their rules.

They pretend they care,
some may actually care,
so they try to help
people like me
learn how to be "socially acceptable".

They may as well say
they are trying to help us
"learn how to be human".

Well that should be
offered to both us and
the neurotypical population.

Socially acceptable is a two way street.
They expect us to act this way

when half the time they themselves
don't even act the way they
are teaching us to be.

But I play by their rules.
Until the day those rules
are able to be changed.

When that day does come,
how to implement the changes
becomes the grand question.

The changes from
the Civil Rights movement
hasn't been implemented
the way Dr. King thought
they would be in nearly sixty years
since the end of the movement.

It will likely take at least
twice as long to bring the changes
both the neurotypical and those like me
for "socially acceptable" two way street
concept to be implemented successfully.

Only Human

I've fallen into a world of darkness
and wondering where I belong.

I'm trying to find my way,
as well as carve a path for others.

I search for answers,
to questions anyone with a
thoughtful mind would ask.

I try to do more than
I may be capable of,
to prove people like me can
do anything ordinary people can do.

I seek to make a mark
upon this world.

Though I likely must face
the fact I'm only human.
I'm not superhuman.

Kids on the spectrum believe that
the Autism itself is a super power.

That is partly true.
The Autism is the foundation
of what our strength is,
but it is up to each of us

to find out what
to build on top of that foundation.

Mine started with Autism,
but has been built into
an ability to craft words that
touch the hearts and minds that
read or hear them.

If that is all I can build,
than I should be satisfied with that.

But I still continue to climb higher.
Even if I fall again,
I would rather fall knowing I tried
than sat around for nothing.

Autism Warrior

I am strong,
I am thick skinned,
if people throw criticism at me now,
their words would ricochet off me.

For I am a honorable warrior,
I know it in my heart.
And no amount of empty words
will change that.

I am Autistic,
and I have come to
accept it and be proud
of what I am.

I am a Autism Warrior.
I fight to prove people like me
are capable of great things.
I also strive
to serve as an example for
the young to look up to.

To show parents and young people
on the Spectrum that
there is hope that they can be more
than what a bunch of old studies claim.

I might be the first,
but I will make sure

I am not the last.

The Long Game

To the parents of autistic kids,
I have something to say to you.

First,
don't give up on them.
They can be taught
on how to be "mainstreamed"
with their neurotypical peers.

Find a behavior technician service.
They have the training and tools
to help them become mainstream.

It's hard to tell how long
it will take to get
the "desirable" results you want.

But never give up on them.
For these services
are like training for a marathon.

You have to practice and train
for weeks or months before
your marathon race.

The training that
the behavior techs give
is essential for
the long run.

You have a kid on the spectrum,
you got to be in it
for the long game
if you want to see the fruits
of the work the technicians put into
the services for your child.

Be patient
and you will see
the miracles
they can perform.

Not a Lost Cause

You need help?
Let me try to help.

Don't tell me
you're a lost cause.

I was called that
in the 90s.

What I know
about people who say
they are a lost cause,
they feel lost.

You are a lost cause
if two conditions are met.

They give up on themselves,
and everyone else
has given up on them.

You accept my help
and you are no longer
lost cause.

You're not a lost cause,
as long as one of us breathes.

I don't abandon

the people I help.

Unwelcomed

We live in a world
that favors those
who are neurotypical.

The general population
usually don't like change.

The only way they accept change
is if it has something to offer them.
Something that benefits them
in one way or another.

We are a change in the population.
That's why it feels like
we are not welcomed by others.

That is why we get picked on
and ignored by others.

Don't take it personal.
There's nothing wrong with you.
They are ignorant.

We have great things to offer,
but it is an exchange.

They help us cope with the world
they make us live in,
and we give them

a remarkable point of view.

Potential breakthroughs in
many different fields of greatness.

The problem with
the general population
is that they want to receive
more than they are willing to give.

Most would rather have
what we can offer first
then give us
the means to thrive
in their world.

The fact is,
they have to give us
the means to thrive,
then we can give
what we have
to offer them.

Most don't want
to even want to negotiate.
They are the ignorant ones
that don't welcome us.

There are some who are
willing to work with us.

They will negotiate
and give us what we need
to thrive in this world.

Among those who are willing,
they will not ask for anything in return.
They are happy to help us.

While some of them
consider helping us
as an investment.

It is hard to determine
their motive a majority of the time.

But once we have
the means to thrive,
we must use our talents
to give back to the population.

That is how we become welcomed,
and how we slowly
push the ignorant out of power.

They Don't Understand

Most neurotypicals
are busy with
their own situation.

Most are lost
in their own little world.

They are all living like
there's no tomorrow.

Yet they criticize
our parents
if we are not acting
the way they think
we should be acting.

If I was a father
of a child on the spectrum,
I would reply

"My apologies.
Their behavior is
a work in progress.

Let me tell you something.
My child is on the spectrum,
and you are more than ignorant.

I would call you

an ignorant bigot.
But that would be
too nice of a label
for me to give you."

As I walk away
with my child,
I would tell my child
"Forgive people like them.
They don't understand us."

One Less Light

They say
"Who cares if
there's one less light
in a sky
of a billion stars?

Who cares if
one more soul
is extinguished?

Who cares if
there's one less light
in this world?"

Well, I certainly do!

Every light,
every soul
is priceless.

If they say
"Who cares if
there's one light
goes out?"

Say
"Well, I do.
Since you have
nerve to say that.

You should be
the one in the abyss
suffering endlessly.

Not the one
you drove
to the point
of ending it all."

You Are Loved

Hey.
You okay?

You feel unlovable,
because of your label
of being on the Spectrum?

That is far
from the truth.

There are many
who do care
whether or not
you are on the Spectrum.

Your label
is meaningless.

It just means
you're different.

You're a rare type of
diamond in the rough.

You just need
some polishing
and some refining.

And know

for a fact,
you are loved.

By a being
beyond understanding,
your family,
and a brother of situation,
that is me.

You should know
that you are
worthy of
true love.

Let me help you,
along with many others
you will meet along the way.

We will help you
get to the point
where you can
open up your wings
and fly as you see fit.

Who to Be

My brothers and sisters,
let me impart
a bit of wisdom.

When it comes to
who you are
and who you are to be,
be someone
you are happy as.

What the neurotypical
or anyone says
about what you should be
doesn't matter.

You should try
several different things.

If one of the activities
pays you and
you enjoy doing it.

You may consider it
as a career choice.

And remember
this phrase:
"You reap
what you sow".

If you put
effort (sow)
into what you do,
you will earn (reap)
rewards for your efforts.

Be the kind of person
that makes you happy.

Perfect

I made mistakes,
several times.

Came through
the fires of life,
scared and burned.

Welcome to
my crazy world.

I have been mistreated,
misunderstood,
and felt abandoned.

But in the eyes
of those who truly mattered
I was good,
they felt I was perfect.

Brothers and sisters,
please listen
and listen well.

No matter what
this world says,
you were made
perfect.

Anyone who say

otherwise
is an ignorant fool.

The world can
be very cruel.

But remember,
no matter what
anyone says,
you are perfect.

You are perfect
to me,
to the grand creator,
and those whom
you call family.

Please
always remember,
you are perfect
to many.

No matter what
this world will say,
you are perfect
to me and
many others.

Halls of Fame

There are many kinds
of the "Hall of Fame".

There's different kinds
of music have Halls,
different sports
have Halls,
there are even
Halls in several schools.

But these halls
are restrictive
and have levels of
bureaucracy.

They require you
to be nominated
by many people
who feel that
you are "worthy".

We,
my brothers and sisters
of situation,
can make a
Hall of Fame
for Autism Success Stories.

An Autism Success Story

is a person on the spectrum
who are doing
the best they can
to be self sufficient
and independent.

You don't need
to be famous.

You don't need
to be athletic.

On a global, national,
or any scale of recognition,
you can be nobody
and still be apart
of this
Hall of Fame.

All we can do
is the best we can.

If you are doing
the best you can
to be self sufficient,
and are happy,
you are already in.

Unsung Heroes

There are many
heroes in the world.

There are
super heroes
that live in
comics and media.

There are
everyday heroes
like those whose
serve and try
to save a life.

But the greatest heroes
are based on
personal perspective.

These heroes
usually don't receive
recognition for
what they do.

These heroes
are called
Unsung Heroes.

To people like us,
the unsung heroes

are the people
who put their
time and energy
into helping us
adapt to the world
we live in.

They put
their personal resources
into helping us thrive.

That's what makes
them heroes.

They make sacrifices
to help us succeed.

Yet,
they get nothing
in return.

The irony is
they don't want anything
in return.

Some will say
"It's my job" or
"It's my pleasure".

When simple gratitude
is they can ask for.

Let's be grateful
for these

unsung heroes.

Why Wait?

There are many groups
that offer us help.

Some are
small grassroot level
organizations or support groups.

Some are capable of
spreading over a large area.
Such as a region or state.

There are very few corporate level
organizations and non profit groups
that span across a nation, nations, or even
around the world.

There are many that are offering
to help us thrive,
but they refuse to work together.

Why?
Why can't we pool resources together
for the good of all on the spectrum?

We all should be on the same side.
We are all on "Team Autism".

Should there be one huge banner
we all are under

with several smaller banners
for each group
who work towards helping us?

Yet it almost looks like
all the groups want to be independent
and are willing to fight each other.

We are working towards the same goal.
Why can't we work together?

Why are we waiting to unite?
What are we waiting for?

Lost and Alone

You try to pretend
your diagnosis
is just a scar
you hide easily.

It is hidden
deep inside you.

It's nothing that
can be fixed
or cured medically.

So you pretend
it doesn't exist.

But this act
doesn't work
forever.

When it finally fails,
you will feel
lost and alone.

It's alright to feel lost,
but you are not alone.

You got a
brother of situation
in me.

I will help
you come to terms
with what you are.

The key difference
between us
and everyone else,
we are potentially
the next phase
of human evolution.

So when the act
finally fails.

Know there's hope
and people who will
welcome you.

Slow Down

Life moves
pretty fast
sometimes.

So you should
slow down
occasionally.

You may miss
something important.

Or a large bulk
of time.

So slow down.

Enjoy life
while you
have time.

Because,
when it comes
time to say
"Farewell"
to everything,
there's no stopping.

No way to turn back
the clock or